Event Planning Ninja

Planning events with 100% success rate

Rachel MacKenzie

RACHEL MACKENZIE

Copyright © 2019 Rachel MacKenzie

All rights reserved.

ISBN: 172210371X
ISBN-13: 978-1722103712

PREFACE

You're planning a summer party, a business breakfast or a conference for several thousand participants with attendees flying in from 6 continents. There are so many things that could go wrong, but they won't! First, because you've got this book in front of you, by the time you're done with reading, you'll surely have a better idea of all the details you should consider. If your event is much smaller and not everything applies, feel free to adjust and pick only the essentials. If, on the other hand, you're planning something really epic, you might need a lot more help in planning and implementing—outsourcing most parts of the work might not be a bad idea. Planning for a small team retreat and planning for a congress is not the same thing, but the same rules apply.

Finally, every event is unique! Even if something doesn't go according to plan, remember: Psst! Nobody noticed. Have fun and celebrate!

At the end of this book you will find a section of my favorite tools: A link to download my event checklist and a budgeting spreadsheet. Make sure you grab them; they are really useful for events of any size.

RACHEL MACKENZIE

EVENT PLANNING NINJA

CONTENTS

	Preface	i
1	Getting Started	1
2	Budgeting for Your Event	Pg 9
3	Event Timeline	Pg 15
4	The Tasty Part	Pg 23
5	Event Entertainment	Pg 27
6	Marketing your Event	Pg 34
7	Resources and Tools	Pg 44
8	About the Author	Pg 45

RACHEL MACKENZIE

GETTING STARTED

Congratulations! Whatever your reason to celebrate, it is surely a good one, and I'm joining you for this occasion. I'm going to walk you through some key decision points for your upcoming event to make sure that nothing has slipped your mind and that, even if you're very busy with a million other things that we all have to do, your event runs smoothly.

Concept is the first milestone to set. What's your Big Day about? Is it a workshop, a speaker event or a party? Well, you probably already know that, or maybe not yet. Now, when you're just starting your planning journey, it's time to decide how big you want your event to be: for a handful of people or on a larger scale. This will influence all other decisions that you'll need to make later on as you go through the planning process, so give it a thought.

The major question to help you make this decision is, "What's the goal of my event?" Do you want to strengthen business relationships, generate leads, create stronger brand awareness, launch a product, promote your services or simply make some money? You may have several goals, but make sure you write them down and articulate them before diving into planning further.

Your event can be linear, non-linear or free flow.

Linear events are one-room conferences and workshops, among others. All participants follow the same timeline from start to finish: opening, coffee break, several sections, and evening reception. Sections can change, but the flow of people doesn't; all of your guests have to fit into the same agenda and space. They are probably the easiest events to organize for you as a host because within the agenda there's very little confusion.

Non-linear events are multiple-venue conferences and trade shows, as an example, where different stakeholders have different interests. You might be hosting several workshops in parallel as well as a stage with presentations. As soon as you have more than one thing happening at the same time, your program needs to be more detailed and your timeline needs to work out for both micro-venues, making sure your key content does not overlap.

Free-flow events are everything from networking parties to festivals and trade shows with no specific timing. Free-flow events can have elements of both linear and non-linear events, but guest experience is even more important when designing a free-flow happening. You've got to make sure your visitors make the most of their time! A great example of a free-flow event is a street food festival, where thousands of people find something to do, although on the surface it might seem that there's no strict agenda.

THE "MORE IS MORE" RULE

More attendees means more opportunities for everyone.

Whether you're planning a business or a private event, a great rule to apply is More Is More. Sometimes 15 key partners or an intimate group of friends that can really bond together is a nice community. I've been at really cozy business lunches, where 12–15 people felt like a family by the end of the event. It's also easier on your budget if you're not planning to monetize it or thinking of a really exclusive format. The downside of having a small group is that you have to hand-pick the guests and manage no-shows really well. Having 3 people skip your celebration when you only invited 10 is different than having the same 3 dropouts when your guest list had more than 50 names on it.

More people means more topics for conversations, a different atmosphere and—essentially—more work for you to plan and implement.

If you don't know the exact number of people you want to invite, give yourself a range and pin a number in the middle of this range: say, 60–80 people, and 70 will be your number to plan for. You will need it for all the preparations, so let's make sure it's in place.

If your party requires complex logistical arrangements, such as flights and accommodation, your estimated number has to be more precise, as everything needs to be booked in advance. However, before you have sent out invitations (or started marketing) and got attendees confirmed, you won't know for sure how many guests are coming. So, to simplify things, let's start with a ballpark number and move on!

I'm expecting to have __100__ guests.

WHY THEY WILL LOVE IT

An event is a long-awaited occasion for both you as a host and your guests —or it should be! If it's your wedding or birthday, the answer to this question is clear—they will love it because you're probably inviting your loved ones who care about you.

What if it's a business occasion? Always make sure there's something for them: networking, great food, loads of learning, you name it. Make sure that your guests go to your event (and don't stay at home watching their favorite movie) and get remunerated for their choice. We always want to spend quality time, and you as event planner take responsibility for the time investment of your guests. This is a great responsibility and you've got to keep in mind the takeaways for your event visitors.

Start planning your event with their goals in mind. Put on the shoes of your attendees and think of the experience you're planning to bring them. If they're coming to network, how are you planning to make them meet the people? If their focus is sales, how is your event going to help them?

They will love the event because __its fun!__

VENUE CHOICE

Venue is a total game changer for the event. It gives the atmosphere and sets the tone, so let's look at the options!

Traditional venues are hotels, conference halls, restaurants, and everything that looks like ... hmm, a traditional event venue. It's pretty easy to distinguish one: they will most certainly have event packages that you can easily adapt to your needs, and they will give you help—for a fee—in hosting and planning your event. By saying traditional, I absolutely don't mean to undermine the great value most of the venues provide. You can make something completely unique in your most-visited hotel. Perhaps uniqueness is not something you're after and focusing on high-quality implementation and less stress is more important for your team. The choice is yours!

Upsides:
- Experience in hosting events and purpose-set facilities
- Option of event planner or event manager to assist you
- Tested subcontractors that you can use
- Equipment for your event will be mostly in place or available for hire

Downsides:
- Sometimes subcontractors are locked-in: even if you really like this rosé wine, you won't be able to bring your own if their catering doesn't allow
- Exclusive venue hire fees might apply

Unconventional venues

Think outside the box: which other cool places in your area do you have that could give your event an interesting touch? If it's a business event, hosting it at a co-working space could give it a trendy touch. If it's a private party, hiring a villa could be your option.

Give your guests a chance to learn, do, hear, see and experience in an unconventional way. At the same time, keep in mind your event objectives and make sure the choice of venue reflects them. If you choose an alternative event venue, make sure you fill it with things, stages, people and objects that reflect your objectives and the values.

Here are a few ideas for unconventional venues that you probably haven't considered yet:

- Parking Lot

There is always a parking lot near the biggest, most expensive venues. Park food trucks in a circle to define the area. You could always set up a band stand for a live band or a DJ in the middle. Add tents and you can host even more people.

- Parking Garages

The top level of most metro parking garages is open and often has the best view of the skyline. Take the same ideas you could use for a parking lot and do them on the top. An added bonus is attendees can park below, eliminating that problem.

- Popular Nightclubs in the Daytime

You'll be surprised, but most of the hottest nightclubs sit empty during the day. You already have all the lighting, sound and food facilities there, plus loads of ambience. And if people are going to be stuck sitting in stack chairs, at least give them an exciting locale. Transform your presenters into content DJs and deliver an "idea mix". Add a real DJ and you can transform a simple luncheon into a spectacular event.

- Been to Art Galleries? Try Art Schools

In galleries, the art is static—finished and on the wall. But art schools are dynamic, active works in progress. In this venue, put your meeting's key content points on canvasses and let the audience physically move from idea to idea. (Thanks to Photoshop, you can take anything you can put on PowerPoint and make it look like art.)

- Warehouses or Converted Spaces

Name it a graffiti party and crash any urban space you have nearby. Ask local graffiti artists to decorate some of the walls with the theme, company name, product, etc. to define the space and the character of the meeting. It can change your party atmosphere and add urban chic to it.

Upsides
- It's going to be an event to remember: unusual venues stick in the memory
- You can customize most parts of the decorations, since you pretty much need to set it up from scratch
- You're in control of the atmosphere

Downsides
- Your budget has to have some flexibility, since pricing is very unpredictable
- Some essential equipment might be missing, be prepared!
- If your venue has never hosted events before, get ready for a long process of explanations
- Permits and regulations need to be checked and sorted out if applicable

VENUE SIZE AND ESSENTIALS

When we hosted an opening party of our office space, at some point in the celebration we managed to fit 75–85 people into 50 square meters, but you clearly don't want to do that. People have bodies. People also appreciate a chance to move around and have some privacy within your amazing event, and generally more space will make your crowd feel more comfortable.

What is too much space? You clearly don't want to give an impression that the event was poorly attended if you have a big warehouse for a handful of people. If we don't take into consideration budgets and the fact that larger spaces in general cost more to hire, this is the only reason for you NOT to take a bigger venue.

If you're working with a traditional event venue, like a hotel, it is almost guaranteed that you will have a good estimate of how many attendees you can fit into the facility. However, if you're taking on a spacious garage, a museum or even an outdoor space, you will need to do calculations yourself. Make sure you know the area of the space. From there on, it's easier.

Here's a rough estimate for the number of people you can fit into your event with different layouts:

SPACE SIZE/ LAYOUT	100 sq. m/ 1077 sq.ft	300 sq.m/ 3330 sq.ft	500 sq.m/ 5380 sq.ft	1000 sq. m/10760 sq.ft
Banquet Style, 60"/72" wide round tables	89/82 ppl	269/248 ppl	448/413 ppl	896/827 ppl
Conference style, attendees sat on all sides	35 ppl	107 ppl	179 ppl	358 ppl
Classroom style, 18"/30" wide desks:	76/63 ppl	230/189 ppl	384/316 ppl	768/632 ppl

Theater style, rows of chairs	Max. 119 people	Max. 358 people	Max. 600 people	Max. 1195 people
Reception style, standing with poseur tables	Max. 119 people	Max. 358 people	Max. 600 people	Max. 1195 people

When talking to your event provider, it's important to clarify these questions:

- What's the timetable of the venue?
- Is any equipment included?
- Can you bring your own equipment or do they have a list of providers they work with exclusively? (If so, it might push your budget towards the higher end)
- Are you allowed to access the venue beforehand to start preparations?
- Is there any storage space available? (You will need it, no matter what type of event you're hosting!)
- What's the parking situation and can you get free passes for organizers and guests?
- Is there any staff that will be assigned to your event to give you and your team a hand?
- What are the extras that are not included in the event hire price?
- Is internet stable and accessible to event guests and organizers?

DATE AND TIME

If your event date is not debatable, feel free to skip this chapter. But if you're still trying to decide when you want to host your event, read on. There are a few considerations that might make your attendance so much higher!

Holidays and "bridges"

Whether it's a fun or business event, you want to be sure it's scheduled for when people are in town. The worst time to plan something is Christmas or Easter weeks, when most of your providers will be more expensive and most of your attendees will be just busy. Make sure you take a close look at the calendar and carefully examine the dates you're picking.

For business events, business days are best. And it doesn't matter whether your guests are business owners or employees, they will appreciate you keeping it within the business week. Their families will surely appreciate that too.

Make sure you take into consideration the business cycles of the attendees. August is really slow for any business in Europe, since everyone enjoys summer vacations. September is the traditional start of business activity. If you're hosting an event for your company, keep in mind internal seasonality. Hosting a team meeting or a conference during the peak sales period is a bad idea because everyone's attention will be away from your event.

Conflicting events

It's not all competition in the events industry. If you're hosting a marketing networking brunch sometime soon and another company is hosting a marketing business breakfast the same week, but earlier than you, you might see some cannibalization. If you're clearly targeting the same audience, they might choose one event or the other. But if you're hosting a marketing networking brunch a week after a large marketing conference, you are in a pretty sweet spot because the attendees of the previous event might want to catch up with each other and strengthen their contacts.

My tip is - if you're just picking the date now, do some research into the events that are already announced and make sure you find a good strategic position on a calendar. Make sure it is not too far from complementary events and not conflicting with your competitors.

BUDGETING FOR YOUR EVENT

Clarity is important from day one of planning. There are a lot of hidden costs to any event, so watch out! Make sure you revise your budget carefully with all the stakeholders because even minor changes—say, having guests arriving 30 minutes earlier—can increase your costs by 5–10%.

GET ORGANIZED

You need to keep your numbers in one place to keep track of them. The easiest way to go about this is to create a simple excel spreadsheet with just a few columns that will show detailed costs and your comments. It will also help you to communicate this information to your partners and other stakeholders when necessary.

Here's an example of what your spreadsheet can look like:

Item	Number of units	Budgeted expense, USD	Actual expense, USD	Comment
Venue rent	1	0		Venue donated by sponsor
Cleaning fees	5	100		Billed hourly by CleanTown
WiFi	2	150		2 hotspots needed

We have also created a complete event budgeting spreadsheet that I use all the time for my events, and you're welcome to download it for yourself. You can find a link to the spreadsheet together with other great free tools in the "Resources" section at the end of this book.

WORKING ON YOUR BUDGET

Items in your list should be as detailed as you can make them. Let's take an example of planning food and drinks. Imagine you've planned overall spending of 300 USD, but now you have decided to add alcoholic drinks too. How do you allocate this money to show how you're planning to spend it?

Having detailed items will also help you to discover hidden costs. Coming back to our food and drinks example, you might see that you need to buy or rent extra utensils, cleaning supplies and table decorations. And within table decorations, you might need flowers or individual table signs. Add it all up.

Number of units

This is another essential column that will show you how many of each item you are planning to have. If you work with a team, having it all on your budget will help you delegate tasks more easily and show the scope. Place details on the document and it will be clear that you need, say, 10 tables, 60 chairs and 30 bottles of wine. When you demonstrate the number of items budgeted for, it also becomes easier to discuss with your co-organizers if your assumptions are correct and whether you're planning to get sufficient amounts for the event. Getting too much can use up your budget too quickly, while getting too little can harm the quality of the event.

Comments

Placing detailed comments is crucial because there you can show the name of your suppliers if you already have them, descriptions of the items and even brands where it's important. Color-coding your budget is another good way of working: mark essentials in green and nice-to-have items in yellow so that you have your priorities in front of you.

Budgeted expenses

You can start as simply as putting a rough ballpark number there. If you don't have a supplier yet, drop a few emails with inquiries as you do your first draft of the budget. The "Better done than perfect" rule applies to your first budget attempt: you can always clarify later.

Actual expenses

You will keep adding these numbers as time goes on, sometimes even after the event. Ideally it's as close to the budgeted expense as you can make it, but life happens, so it's better to keep track of your expenses for you to learn from.

WHAT TO BUDGET FOR

Here are a few budget lines that might come in handy for your document. Expand them to include more details if needed.

Food and drinks

If your event has any food included, what's the minimum you will pay for catering irrespective of the number of guests? What are the service fees? Does your catering service provide staff at an additional cost? Are the drinks served at a bar, and if yes, how many bars do you need? How are the bars equipped? Are they cash bars or bartender bars? Are gratuities included? Do you have tables, chairs and decorations for the above? Some catering companies provide them for a fee, and some venues already have all of that pre-installed. If you need to hire any equipment to seat your guests, make sure you know how many items you're lacking.

Travel costs

If you need to travel to your event, make sure to include travel costs and accommodation for your entire team. Once you land, what's the price of a return taxi ride to the venue? How much is the cost of additional meals for your team for the duration of the event? Estimate the costs per day.

Venue rentals

What's the timetable of your venue and how far in advance can you access it to make your preparation is smoother? What's the damage deposit and how much can you be charged if any damage from your side happens?

Event marketing

What's the overall budget and how is it distributed between different platforms? Are you publishing your event on a variety of event platforms, and if so, what are their ticketing charges? Are you using an agency, and if so, what's their cost in addition to the ad spend? For an agency, it's okay to leave a rough ballpark of 20–30% on top of your budget, but it can vary depending on your location and their scope of work.

Do you have branding for your event in place or do you need to hire a graphic designer to work on that? If so, you might consider including an event brand book and a number of visuals, from banners to decorations onsite.

Audiovisuals

Make sure you make decisions on what items are absolutely must-haves, like sound and a DJ if you're planning a themed pool party. For the same type of event, lights and screens might be a great addition, but you can do well without, especially if it's a daytime party.

Before you sign, thoroughly read your agreement with an A/V provider: are there any damage fees? What extra costs could you incur?

Photo and video production

Do you have full copyrights of the material used during the event? How soon can you expect it to be ready and can you have all raw pictures and footage or only edited versions? How big is the team of photographers and videographers working with you? Do you need any special equipment, like a press-wall? Do they need an assistant from the side of organizers to help them shoot video interviews with the participants? If so, assign a dedicated person because photo and video production is an extremely important investment you can use for your future events and promos, and, if it's implemented well, it can boost your business.

Plan B for everything

Make sure you outsmart the bad luck. Anything can go wrong, so think of the absolutely worst case scenario and make a few additions to your budget. If the weather is not great and your event is outdoors, can you pull up a tent or distribute umbrellas? I normally add 10–15% on top of the final budget to plan for emergencies, and sometimes they happen.

Think of cancellation fees: if you had to change the date of your event or cancel it completely, what would it cost you?

Hopefully, by now your budget is close to being complete! However, there are always items to add and hidden fees that you can discover along the way. On a conclusive note, review our list of hidden costs—do any of them apply to you?

21 HIDDEN COSTS FOR YOUR EVENT PLANNING BUDGET:

- Additional attendees and walk-ins
- Amenities
- Attrition
- Conference Calls
- Corkage
- Credit card processing fees
- Event marketing platforms
- Housekeeping
- Insurance for the event
- Signage
- Audiovisual (i.e. power strips, power, flipcharts)
- Office supplies and shipping charges
- Onsite hourly staffing charges
- Room drops
- Service charges
- Staff expenses onsite
- Taxes
- Tips and gratuities
- Website and web design
- Wi-Fi Access
- Wire transfer fees

THE DOS AND DON'TS OF YOUR EVENT BUDGET

Let's start with the DOs of creating your event budget:

- DO create a line in your spreadsheet for every single detail. Even small costs add up to an important chunk of your expenses
- DO plan for a "rainy day", sometimes even literally. You should have your backup plan in case murphy's law applies to your event day
- DO know your deadlines because missing them can cause you extra costs
- DO request budgets from multiple suppliers and compare them in advance
- DO know what's important to spend on and what is a commodity that nobody will notice (hence, you can cut a corner and buy the most

basic item)
- DO look into budgeting software if your event is very complex or large-scale

The DON'Ts of budgeting your event:

- DON'T assume best-case scenario
- DON'T make your numbers look too good because you will end up overspending or under delivering
- DON'T choose the cheapest option for every item: it's worth investing when it comes to creating memorable events
- DON'T postpone creating your budget. It's one of the first things you should start working on when planning an event

EVENT TIMELINE

It's too easy to miss an important deadline when you've got so much on your plate. That's why I recommend getting organized from the very beginning and setting an event timeline that will have a go-to spreadsheet that will remind you of the due dates of specific action items. Prioritizing is a key because delaying specific parts of your process can limit your choices and even cost you money, as in the case of delaying payments.

In the "Resources" section at the end of this book you can find a link to a pre-made spreadsheet that we use for planning mid- to large-scale events. It's a pretty handy visual tool, and we left our values in there so that you could just edit and customize them according to the needs of your event.

WHEN SHALL I START?

In most cases, 6 months is a good notice period for mid-size events, but if you're planning a festival, a concert, a major conference or anything of a large scope, it's not rare to start planning a year in advance.

6 MONTHS IN ADVANCE

That's when you put your ducks in a row; decide on the type and the scope of the event. One of the first things to do is **define a core team** involved in planning and implementation. You will need strong support because you will need to make micro-decisions on daily basis, so make sure the core team is onboarded from day one. You will need to decide on communication tools (say, event-specific Slack channel or anything you're already using for your team). Define roles and responsibilities because when you have specific sectors where you trust one another's opinion, it will be much easier to move on with the event planning.

Now you have a team in place, let's **develop the timeline** and set core milestones for all of you. Mark core meetings on it and make sure you're on track. Add key events to a shared calendar, you will be more productive working towards a day when you need to report to your peers.

Make your budget
Start working on it as soon as you can. We gave a thorough overview of budgeting in the previous chapter, so revise our tips and tools if necessary, create a shared file and keep adding items to your first draft if you feel that something is missing. It's better to over prepare than under deliver, remember?

Select the venue and book it
Securing the venue is crucial because other decision points will be related to the type of space you have, amenities, facilities and location. So don't underestimate the urgency of having your space booked; secure your first option before it's gone.

Book key providers
These include your speakers, your A/V provider, catering and entertainment. Collaborating with the above works great in the process of selecting a venue, too; sometimes AV team and catering team will help you to access the venue to determine whether it's fit for your purpose. Don't be afraid of asking your potential partners about alternative venue locations, they might surprise you with something you haven't considered yet.

Define marketing strategy
You might create an amazing event, but it won't be successful if you don't attract a sufficient volume of attendees. Event marketing is necessary for all types of events: even if you're hosting a team reunion, the buzz around it should keep people excited and eager to attend; if you're hosting a festival, you have to build the name and the brand.

What type of promotion are you planning and when? Is it paid advertising, and if so, where? Do you need to get in touch with the influencers to promote your event? If you opted in for an event website, make and launch it now and add more information and updates as you have it clear.

Reach out to potential sponsors
If your event is dependent on sponsorship support, you should have a clear sponsorship strategy in place and that's the point in time when you've

got to start implementing it. Bear in mind that you're depending on their marketing budgets, and as much as they are interested in supporting you and your event, sometimes they need time to prepare. We will talk more about sponsors in the chapter on marketing, but meanwhile keep a track of this to-do item.

3 MONTHS IN ADVANCE

Publish agenda

Your event agenda, including the names and the bios of the speakers, should be out by now. Make sure you reach out to them to confirm the details of their talks and participation details. If you have many speakers on board, having one contact person from your team as a "speaker relations manager" is very helpful. In most cases, you will need to request from your speakers:
- Bio
- Topic and a short description
- Headshot
- Travel and accommodation confirmation

Connect with your AV team

Make sure you know what format the presentations should be in, what type of cables will be needed to connect laptops and other equipment, whether they provide all of it or if you need to place a separate order to another provider.

Book remaining suppliers

It's now time to book your decorators and cleaning team, if needed, recruit volunteers and order everything from stationery to swag and signage. If you haven't budgeted for something, it's also time to review your budget, but hopefully you prepared well and none of the items are coming as a surprise. Even though it seems a little early, it's important to order supplies 3 months in advance to allow time for international shipments and production. Having to pay extra for urgency will definitely come at an extra cost, so it's far better to plan beforehand.

ONE MONTH TO GO!

Create a detailed timeline of the event day

Your public agenda is important, but the behind-the-scenes flow is critical. You have to know what time and when the supplies are in place, when the speakers and catering arrive, as well as the work of all of your staff, from meet-and-greet to departure procedure. Everything you've been working on is visualized within the few hours of the event, and if you don't put enough effort into this, you can appear underprepared.

Set up a meeting with your key providers

It's ideal that you have a meeting with all of your providers and discuss the process of the setup of the event day. If your venue is available a day in advance, you might be able to start setting up earlier, but I wouldn't assume this without definite confirmation from the venue. Share a detailed plan of the event day with all of the stakeholders, making sure you're all on the same page.

Finalize the catering order

One month before the event day you probably already have the exact number of attendees and can finalize the catering order. According to your contract, the final day for changes can vary, so set a reminder to communicate the last minute changes in the last possible day.

Create emergency plan

Your emergency plan is something that you and your team should take seriously. Talk through a variety of possibilities and make sure you eliminate at least some of the risks associated with running your event. Discuss security matters, weather factors, force-majeure circumstances and any emergency that could occur. What if your keynote speaker is late? What happens if you have a high cancellation ratio? Having a contingency plan will make you feel at peace and empower your team to action in case anything surges.

Communicate with your speakers

Make sure you have all the requested information from all of them, confirm their travel and accommodation details and request a copy of the speeches and/or presentations.

Finalize sponsorship opportunities

You might still onboard a couple of minor sponsors now, but one month before the event is pretty much the deadline for your sponsors to get on board. Now you should already know who's on board and follow up with them to confirm sponsorships and underwriting.

Publicity and media

Release press announcements about keynote speakers, celebrities, VIPs attending, honorees, etc. Do write a personalized email to top journalists in your sector. Even if you don't speak to them in person, it's your last chance to start building this relationship.

Post your initial event news release on your website and circulate to all partners, affiliated organizations, etc.

ONE WEEK AHEAD

Develop a master plan
Have all event organizers meet and confirm all details against your master plan, ensuring all backup plans are developed for any situation (e.g., backup volunteers as VIP greeters, additional volunteers for registration or setup, etc.).

Finalize the event script
The timeline of the day of the event should be as detailed as you can make it because you will need to brief all hosts, greeters, and volunteers about their event duties and timelines. Send out copies of your event script to your team and anyone involved in event implementation to ensure a smooth process.

Develop signage
Now that you have a definite attendee list, it's time to finalize your final seating plan, place cards and venue signage. This seems like a small task, but don't leave it till the last moment. Ensure all promo items, gifts, plaques, and trophies are onsite and you've got it all branded.

Make print and online copies of any speeches, videos, presentations, etc.

Communicate numbers to catering
Don't miss any diet preferences: your catering staff should know the estimated number of special meals requested, so be very specific.

Attendee checklist
Do the final registration check, name badges and registration list. Ensure registration and media tables are prepared and stocked with necessary items (e.g., blank name badges, paper, pens, tape, stapler, etc.).

Confirm media attending
Determine photo and interview opportunities with any presenters and VIPs and confirm details with interviewees and media. Use these opportunities as your invitation letters to the media and confirm their attendance (you might need more than just one email).

THE DAY OF THE EVENT

Planning the flow of your event day is crucial because that's where the attendee experience is created. What is she going to feel, see, and hear? What is she going to learn? Who is she going to meet?

My best advice is put yourself in the shoes of your event guest and imagine his experience from minute one. How are you going to be moving across the event venue as soon as you arrive? What do you do first, and where do you go after? As an event attendee, what's the most important memory you're going to be sharing with your friends and colleagues about this day?

Let's see what items you might add to your event day timeline to ensure you have it all covered:

Setup.
Buffer at least a couple of hours for your team to set up on the day of the event before you open the doors. If you're planning a large-scale event, this will mean that all the preparations are finished days before, but you still need to get there early; there are always last minute items you as hosts will need to take care of.

Meet and greet.
Give your attendees some time to settle, allow time for registration, swag distribution and let them get familiarized with the venue and agenda.

Speakers.
You should have an exact timeline for each speaker: the start, the finish of their presentation and some buffer time in between to allow for transitions.

Meals and breaks.
Communicate with your catering team about the meal start and finish times.

Event end time.
Even if you have a late night cocktail reception or a party at the end of your event, it can't last forever, so make sure you have a time in place for when the lights are on.

Clean-up.
Set up a plan for your cleaning team to ensure you clean the venue up by the time your rental period is over. Make sure you leave a buffer time in between the event end time and the clean-up too.

On a final note, don't take too many responsibilities upon yourself as an organizer because it's important to have someone taking care of the "flow" of the event. Don't worry, you will be busy anyway. The best event is the one that runs by itself and you can just step back and enjoy it too!

AFTER THE EVENT

Now, when the fun part is over, the work is not. Follow-up is as important as preparation.

Debriefing
Schedule a debriefing meeting with your team and host it the right way. The day after the event is the right time to do it: try to overcome the need to get some break time because it's important to get everyone's fresh impressions and thoughts.

Set up a board (a whiteboard or a text document will both work well) and take notes, making sure that you covered the following topics: key successes, struggles and pain points, complaints, space for improvements and lessons learnt. Store this document for yourself and make sure you go through it next time you're hosting an event.

Do your numbers
If you followed my tips and did your numbers in the budgeting table, it's time to open the document again and add up all of the expenses, including the ones that happened during the event day and right after. Check with the venue if you used any of your damage deposit and take into consideration extra hours billed by any of the providers. Compare your budgeted expenses with the actual ones and take note.

Acknowledge everyone
Send your thanks yous and acknowledgement letters to speakers, volunteers, donors, media, sponsors and partners. Include a link to pictures and videos if relevant. Events are a lot about building relationships, so make sure you're on top of the game.

Store materials and data
Here's what you might want to keep after the event, since it makes up part of your learning and experience for all future event planning.

- Financial status, including all receipts and documentation. It's not only necessary for your accountant but also might contain costs breakdown—an invaluable piece of data for future planning. If you have this information, budgeting for your next events can be easy as 1-2-3: just take a look at the hourly rate and equipment costs and multiply to new variables. It's really handy to get the 1st draft of your numbers before getting more details from providers.

- Registration data and contact details. Your attendees will appreciate event follow-up at some point, maybe some links to post-event materials like video recordings or photos. It will keep them engaged and loyal to you and your brand and strengthen your relations. But to send them anything, you need to organize the contact data.

- Marketing report. If you did your event marketing by yourself, spend a couple of hours writing major takeaways on this. If you hired an agency, request one from them. It's critical to know how your marketing investment played out, what was successful and what was a waste of resources. You want to see your spending across various marketing channels vs. the number of attendees that came from these channels (if it's possible to track, of course—you won't know if you had 10 billboards, for example). But the more you can measure the more efficient your future spending will be.

Opportunity development

Any event makes an open door to more opportunities. So, last but not least, make sure you capture yours and take care of the new contacts, potential partners and proposals. Prioritize this task and don't let it slip away from you as you're very busy with post-event hassle.

THE TASTY PART
OR FOOD AND DRINKS AT YOUR EVENT

While planning food and drinks, always refer back to the event schedule. Take as rule #1 that you can't keep your attendees hungry or thirsty because that will create the most long-lasting memory about your event.

Hence, while planning a half-day event, plan for a minimum of one break time and ensure some snacks are served.

Even if the food and drinks are not included in the event price, make sure you've got enough food stands, bars and other spots for your visitors to take a bite. The worst logistical nightmare I've seen is a 3000-people conference and one food stand that ran out of supplies during the first hours.

PLANNING A MENU

The type of food you're serving depends on how much time and when exactly you're willing to dedicate to meals.

The longest lasting menu items are normally selected for business breakfasts and lunches, since guests might take turns over an extended period grabbing something to eat.

Menu planning is one of the most important items on your event to-do list. Always defer to culinary professionals who possess the necessary food knowledge to ensure your guests leave the event praising your creative menu. Even if the focus of your event is far from food, menu is the factor that can't go unnoticed, especially if it's mediocre to poor. So if you can't afford quality food on your budget, maybe consider including basic part of it—at a high standard—on the house and some part of the menu for a fee.

Since in the business world events frequently are built around food offerings, it's important to keep the menu practical.

THE BIG THREE +

Breakfasts

Most caterers will offer you standard options of breakfast, lunch and dinner with some flexibility on your side. Breakfast is probably most practical in its packaged option, since breakfasts at the events generally require little innovation and just create a "soft landing" for all of your arrivals and a networking space. So take a look at sweet pastries, hot buffets, brekky stations and go ahead selecting the ones you like most and the ones that work well with your budget. You will need this energy further on to make choices on lunch and dinner, and breakfast can just go with the flow.

Type of meal	Duration
Buffet	1–3 hours
Box lunch	30-min break
Plated meal	90 min
Cocktail reception before dinner	1 h
Cocktail reception solo	1,5–3 h

Lunches

Buffet lunches or boxed lunch? The choice will totally depend on your event schedule. Ask your caterer for options and make sure there's sufficient time to accommodate it.

Dinner

The most important meal of your event is definitely dinner. If it's in your schedule, your guests will be expecting to be impressed or at least surprised, so don't let them down. The big question you have to ask yourself is whether you and your audience will be content with a buffet dinner or if a plated service is a better choice. The latter requires 1,5–2 hours of time, while a buffet can be done within 1 h.

Break meals

If you're hosting a multi-day conference, your caterer will most likely present you with an option of break meals, which are normally packaged, and reception options that can go together with hot platter stations and dessert stations. Both reception meals and breaks are normally charged per hour per person and in very rare circumstances per consumption.

Special needs

It's generally not a bad idea to conduct a survey of menu preferences to minimize waste and make all of your guests feel welcome. You should consider planning for:

Special diet requirements (vegetarian, vegan, celiac, sugar-free, no lactose etc.)

Religious requirements (halal, Hindu, Lent etc.)

Other special menus (kids, babies, no alcohol etc.)

It doesn't mean that all of the above options have to be present, but you can definitely derive the most critical ones from the demographics of your attendees and make adjustments accordingly.

HOW MUCH TO ORDER

You as a host definitely don't want to find yourself in a situation where the food ran out 2 hours earlier than it was supposed to! Here's a quick rule of thumb from us on how to estimate the amounts yourself.

Beverages

Hot beverages and juices are normally ordered by liters or gallons, depending on where you are located. If you're hosting an event in Europe or the US, it's pretty safe to assume that 70% will drink coffee, 20% will prefer decaf and 10% drink tea and infusions.

Depending on the size of the cup, there are 3–6 cups of coffee per liter (or 12–20 cups per gallon). You can always ask about the size of the cup of your caterer or venue and make your estimates.

For breakfast, we generally plan on 2 cups of hot beverage per person. Hence, for 100 attendees, assuming 16 cups per gallon/4 cups per liter, we will need:

9 gallons/35 liters of coffee
2.5 gallons/10 liters of decaf
2 gallons/7,5 liters of hot water for tea

For morning and afternoon breaks, we use these ballparks:
- Regular coffee - attendance x 50%
- Decaf coffee - attendance x 25%
- Tea - attendance x 20%

Appetizers

Estimate 10–15 pieces per guest at an event that does not include dinner. Plan a little more for buffet style service since guests tend to eat more from a buffet than they eat off hand-passed trays. If appetizers are followed by salad and main, lower the number to 3–4 per person. Midday snacks only require between one and three appetizer pieces per guest.

Main dish

If your event is hosted at a hotel or at a venue with a fully-equipped kitchen, it's totally safe to order plated meals for your attendance x 90%. You don't want to overcommit resources, and there are always cancellations and no-shows. However, if your event is off the grid and additional meals can't be created, it's maybe safer to order precise numbers.

A rough estimate for your perfect entrée size (protein like beef, pork, chicken, or seafood) should be between five and seven ounces or 150–200 grams. Two or three sides cover the plate without causing guests to overindulge. The combination of side dishes includes a choice of beans, rice, pasta, fresh vegetable or some form of potatoes.

Remember that most sit down dinners come with bread and salad, which rounds out the perfectly planned event menu.

Bar

Plan on providing one bartender per every 75–100 guests. If you're providing a cash bar, 50% of the guests will attend; if you're providing a hosted bar, closer to 75% of attendees will participate. Estimate about 2,5 drinks during the first hour of the event. If you're providing wine, it's good to keep in mind that 1 bottle equals about 5 glasses.

However, the best data to rely on is your own historical data because certain audiences have specific preferences and consumption patterns, so make sure this time, when you host your event for the first time ever, you record all of this handy data.

EVENT ENTERTAINMENT

Again, depending on the size and the scope of your event, the appropriate entertainer may vary from Kylie Minogue to a local tribute band. Although it's much easier to win your audience with a famous and demanded entertainer, there are always hidden gems and great ideas even if you need to impress without having to spend a Grammy-level budget.

HOW TO CHOOSE AND FACTORS TO CONSIDER

First and foremost, take into consideration the tastes and preferences of your audience. It's probably everyone's top-1 mistake assuming your customers have the same tastes as you. Nope. They don't. Maybe they are 20–30 years older than you, and your stars are unknown in their community. Think of what they love, what other events they go to and what "theme" might suit them best.

The focus of your event is the second most important factor. Do you remember that in the very beginning of your event planning journey we were talking about your Why and What? What is that one thing that your guests will remember when they are back at home? If it's business contacts, great, keep your focus on making sure your entertainment has a strong "social component", from bars and lounges to appropriate table arrangements. If you want them to remember the show and the event atmosphere, that's where you have to invest more time and energy.

If food and menu is your focus, dedicate time to planning it. Where the focus goes energy flows. You have to keep in mind your goal as an organizer and work on achieving it every day of your event planning period.

HOW MUCH DOES THE FUN COST?

That's a great question. Unfortunately, the worst idea to help you answer this question is to google. You can get the lowest possible price for really basic things, but picking entertainment by price is an even worse idea than googling the level of prices. Anyway, let's see what data we can get here!

There are two important things to know:

1. An entertainer for a closed private event will cost more than an entertainer for a public one.

Why? Because public events can provide some publicity and PR opportunities that normally come together with further opportunities. Hence, if you're hosting a private party, get ready for a higher budget, but if you're planning a large-scale event, know that you can negotiate here.

2. The entertainer's fee is just the top of the iceberg. Show setup costs and other expenses are the underwater part of it.

Wait, what did you just say? Hidden costs? Exactly. These can be lower or non-existent with a general profile artist, but if you're serious about getting a celebrity, be also serious on the budget side. First, travel costs come as part of the performance fee. You're expected to cover the travel and lodging costs of the artist and her crew since they never travel alone. Oh, and you're not in a position to negotiate that, I'm afraid. Equipment setup and other minor expenses go without saying! It's normally all outlined in a rider, so read it well.

NEGOTIATE LIKE A PRO

First of all, don't plan your event with the idea of a specific entertainer in mind. As we mentioned before, it's really difficult to find out current market prices for specific personas, so you've got to be flexible.

Second of all, get ready to negotiate because this is the norm in this industry. Reach out to the agent and be consistent with a follow-up. If they didn't reply in the first instance, email/call again in several days. You have to demonstrate interest from your side if your target is a celebrity. Again, that's just how things work in this industry. I wouldn't recommend reaching out to more than 2–3 targets at once because your plan A might as well be available, and you don't want to get involved in a number of negotiations.

So, time for your first offer! If you've never done this before, there's nothing to worry about. Start with offering 10–15% lower than what you think could be their current price. If it was several digits lower than their current expectations, they will probably never reply again. In all other cases you should expect a little bit of a back-and-forth in the negotiations process, hopefully settling at your initial number+10–15%.

Make sure you know when to efficiently walk out of the negotiations. Your budget should be in place as well as all the details of your event. This way you will know your exact spending limits. And don't worry if plans A and B (and C!) fell through, there's always someone out there who you haven't thought of yet, but they will provide an excellent experience for your people on the day of the event.

20 EVENT ENTERTAINMENT IDEAS YOU HAVEN'T TRIED YET

If you pick one or a series of smaller entertainment ideas as opposed to hiring a major star performer, there's so much you can try and experiment with! We could have created a whole book covering entertainment ideas only, but since that's not our focus, we've picked 20 top ideas and leave you with them as a thought-starter. If you're missing more options, social media can be a great source of inspiration. Dive into pinterest or any other social media of your choice.

To make the choice easier, we tagged these options with approximate pricing:
low <$200
medium $201 – $5000
high >$5000

1. Hire a street artist
Price range: low to medium
Maybe even literally. There are so many hidden gems that you haven't considered out there. A creative business www.bookastreetartist.com has a great collection of artists across all of Europe. There are similar projects in

the US and other locations, and prices are really competitive.

2. Set up a casino table
Price range: medium
Regardless of the size of your event, poker or roulette or a blackjack setup will be appreciated by many; it's a rather quiet activity, inviting attendees to socialize, and it's surely something different. Whether you choose to set up one table or several, your guests will be kept busy for quite some time, so make sure the bar is open until late!

3. Create an art gallery
Price range: medium
When was the last time you tried painting? Maybe never really. What if you bring plenty of material and let the magic flow? Let your guests get creative, maybe set a drawing topic—a theme of your event or your brand—and watch them visualizing it.

Some help from a professional artist is always great, but they can make the work themselves. For the rest of the night your new art gallery can be positioned on one of the walls. It will definitely be everyone's favorite picture spot!

4. Back to teenagehood
Price range: medium
Computer games are a luxury for many because we just don't have time to spend playing, not anymore. Let your audience release their inner child; hire a few game stations and see what happens. From old-school Super Mario to Wii consoles, there are plenty of ideas for you to implement. Maybe your game theme can be "Favorite games from the '90s" or just first computer games. If you're more of a futurist, take a look at the recent releases!

5. Laugh together
Price range: medium
Everyone likes good jokes. The best ones are remembered and repeated! Think of inviting a stand-up comedian to your party and charging the atmosphere with some good laughter. Some of them can create a custom show for you that will fit the atmosphere and the context or customize one of their shows for your audience. Prices vary, but a custom show starts at USD 2500.

6. Motivational speakers
Price range: medium to high
Invite a motivational speaker to kick-off your morning sessions. Since

TED talks gained popularity, we all got hooked on motivational boosts every now and then. A speaker can boost the energy of your conference attendees and set the right mode. Beware of prices: some speakers can charge as high as celebrities for an appearance at your event. But if you sign a niche celebrity for the speech, you can win the love of your audience for the rest of the event.

7. Let the spirit flow!
Price range: medium
If you're hosting a bar during the evening, you can also set a cocktail making experience and teach your guests to make their perfect margaritas, mojitos or Bloody Mary. Brand it all with your company logo on cocktail decoration preps, and create loads of picture-perfect content for your future promotion on social media.

8. Sommelier in the house
Price range: low to medium
For a more sophisticated touch to your event, create a wine-tasting game and try to guess the origin, the flavors and the age of the wine. Blind-tasting will create some good laughs; try to estimate the price by the flavor! And to add a bigger theme to the wine tasting, add some French starters and wine-cellar-styled decorations.

9. Say cheese!
Price range: medium
A photo booth is such an easy choice because ... it works! An interesting twist to your booth is instantly printing magnets with the pictures so that your guests have a lasting memory of your event at their home or office kitchen. Include branded frames with the pictures with your contact data if it's suitable, and the booth will generate you some business for years to come. Remember, your event is made to create long-lasting relationships and foster the old ones.

10. Digital caricatures
Price range: low to medium
Pen and pencil ages are gone long ago! Nobody will really hang their portraits in their office or dining hall, but they might use them on social media if an artist gets a chance to email them the piece of art they created instantly. That's some additional buzz going towards your event—isn't it what we all are looking for?

11. Corporate percussion
Price range: medium
These work best at an open-air venue. Percussion shows are a total hit

for any size event. You will need to hire a professional band to create the experience for you. A high-energy show in which your invitees participate is an amazing addition to your program.

12. iPad Magician
Price range: medium
For technology and gadget lovers/events, iPad magicians are the perfect act to amaze and entertain your guests. iPad magicians perform bespoke shows for the digital age, and many high-profile brands and events are eager to experience this unique brand of magical entertainment.

13. Interactive wait staff
Price range: medium to high
Embedded in the canvas of your catering, interactive wait staff is great for smaller venues, especially if you're lacking a stage and performance area. Performance is not limited to singing and dancing staff. They could be impersonators, rollerbladers or wearable tables, all serving food and drinks while interacting with guests. Ideas like this work great as conversation starters as well as memorable pieces to take home and talk about.

14. Sand artists
Price range: medium
If you've never seen a sand show it's worth checking out! A group of artists will create sand animations live, telling a story with moving sand. A memorable experience will definitely create a wow-factor for your guests, and it is still not overused in the corporate events arena.

15. Gamify your event
Price range: low to medium
There's plenty of event tech at your disposal to gamify pretty much any part of it. Reward specific behaviors that you want to encourage: allocate points for visiting stands, interacting with each other or taking part in the event activities. It will work much better if you have a giant leaderboard installed in the main area of the event. As a nice addition to the contest, you can give your attendees an option of a prize or a donation to a charity of their choice.

16. Quiz
Price range: low
Use your breaks and technical pauses to entertain your attendees and release some fun and good energy. Run a quick quiz in between your official sessions. It doesn't have to have heavyweight content; find out if you have more taco or pizza lovers, more night owls or early birds, more rock or rap fans, and instantly show results on the screen. They will surely talk about it

during the coffee break!

17. Live stream
Price range: low to medium
Depending on the profile of your speaker and whether he is willing to do a talk for free,

if you don't have the budget to bring an influential speaker of your choice, you can livestream her! This generally works great if the ratio of live streams and in-person talks is correct. Make sure you pick a charismatic and experience moderator. It's even better if it's someone your audience knows well.

18. -Athons
Price range: low
Turn a lengthy event into productive fun with a hackathon, designathon or any other -athon you can think of! You can adapt these to your industry and they are more intense than a roundtable or breakaway, and everyone focuses on working together to achieve a common goal.

19. Speed networking
Price range: low
If your event has more than 50 attendees and most of them will be meeting each other for the first time, this is a great format to make the most out of the newly established connections. Take dating out of the equation and build relationships quickly with speed networking designed to ignore those awkward moments. You will need a bell, a timer and business cards. Make participants meet each other within 30 seconds—and move! Ask about sectors and industries that could be relevant and note who to talk to at the mixer afterwards. An excellent ice breaker and a quick way to find who is important to you!

20. Inaugurate a mural
Price range: medium to high
This works best if you're hosting an event at a venue you own (your home office, HQ or company-owned facility). Commission artwork or have a mural created in honor of your event. It could contain your branding and what makes your business special or stand out as well as key features that define you. Fancy a casual style? Make it in graffiti!

MARKETING YOUR EVENT

You've gone that far. You have created an unbelievably cool concept, onboarded a great team, solved loads of logistic puzzles and invested a lot of energy in this event. Yet everything could be a total waste of time and other invaluable resources if you skip this part.

Now, let's take it seriously and start talking about marketing your event. To be honest, this chapter could have been #1 in importance, but we're placing it at the very end on purpose: you have to remember it best.

If you are reading this book in paper version, do highlight action items. If you've got an e-book, use your kindle tools to take notes and highlight parts that are relevant for you. Marketing your event at the right time to the right audience is your key to success!

We're going to cover these topics:
1. Event marketing goals
2. Metrics and measuring event success
3. Event marketing channels
4. Event website and SEO
5. Promoting your event on social media
6. Landing event sponsors

Let's go!

EVENT MARKETING GOALS

If your event is a friendly get-together, you might not need any metrics because you'll probably estimate success by your gut feeling—whether you and your dearest had a good time. But if it's a business happening, gut feeling is not enough. Let's revise the S.M.A.R.T. acronym and define your event marketing goals.

Specific - the more precise you are in defining your event goals the higher your chances of achieving them. Ask yourself very specific questions about your desired outcome and try to come up with detailed answers. You need something better than, "It has to be amazing."

Measurable - use numbers and exact figures to define your event success. Is it a number of registrations? Is it revenues? Is it a number of leads and opportunities created? Is it the feedback received? Attach an exact number to all of your variables.

Achievable - set a high plank, but make sure you can still get there; otherwise the motivation of your team can drop. Try setting two goals - level 1 and level 2, maybe even give them names, say, 3-star goals and 5-star goals where 5-star goals seem slightly high but you think you have 10% chance of reaching them.

Results-oriented - it's important to measure the final results, not the process of getting there. It's helpful to invite 100 companies to attend your trade show, but it's even more important to have the 10 first participants signed 6 months before the event date. Focus on actual outcome.

Time-bound - create deadlines for every event goal and stick to them. How will your goals develop over time? Say, how many attendees to you want to have registered 3 months before? 1 week before? 1 day prior to your event?

METRICS AND MEASURING EVENT SUCCESS

1. Registrations

This is the most obvious and basic metric that you should definitely look at. However, there's so much more to it than just the number of people registered to attend. You can get a lot more insight if you're able to get data from your ticketing or event tech platform: what month was peak for registrations and what marketing channel were they brought in by? What ticket type was most popular among attendees?

2. Revenues

This is another essential metric of success if you're running a paid event. But again, don't stick to the final number and try to dig deeper to reveal more factors behind it. Which ticket type was sold most? What was the average price per paying attendee? What was the demographic of your attendees? All of this data can be drawn out of the revenues.

3. Cost to revenue ratio

Total numbers are not important if they are not compared to each other. What's your revenue in comparison to cost? This metric is more important if the goal of the event is profit. A simple way to set this metric is to take your budgeted costs and compare them with your sales estimates.

4. Attendee engagement

Tackling attendee engagement is very valuable because it can indicate if your event was a right fit for the audience and whether it was a good investment of resources. Events are in essence about building relationships, so monitoring the above can demonstrate if this goal has been accomplished.

5. Attendee satisfaction

Your best judges are your event guests. Everything you are planning is done to please them, and you need to learn your lessons about what makes them happy. Run a survey and ask them one or more short and specific questions by the end of the event. My favorite is NPS - Net Promoter Score. You're asking only one question: On a score of 0 to 10, how likely are you to recommend this event to your friend? 0–5 are detractors, 6–7 are neutrals and 8–10 are promoters. Calculate your NPS with a simple formula:

% Promoters - % Detractors = Net Promotion Score

6. Social media mentions

Hashtags and mentions build your event brand over time. Over 98% of event attendees create digital content about events, almost 100% post about them. Your role is to maximize your reach, maximizing the long-lasting marketing effect of social media. There are many tools to monitor it, and the first way to do so is to create a custom event hashtag and promote it at the event.

7. Attendee numbers

The number of registrations doesn't always match the number of actual attendees, especially in case of free events, where dropout rates can be as high as 70–80%. Ideally you don't get to this ratio, but it's always important to record check-ins and demographics of your attendees.

8. Customers acquired

If your event was created as a marketing platform, this is the crucial metric to consider. Several conversions might happen sometime later, but with the right technology you can still identify the source of the leads as the event itself. Tackling this metric will help you to attribute spending directly to the revenues generated by the event and draw further conclusions.

9. Sponsorship satisfaction

Looking to land more and bigger sponsors? Make sure you take care of the first backers and record the data. You can do it in several ways: conducting a debriefing meeting or sending out a survey. You should get an answer to the question of what worked best for them and what didn't.

EVENT MARKETING CHANNELS

Before you start your event marketing campaign, let's talk about one crucial decision: marketing channels that you will focus on. There's a common idea that every little helps and that you should talk about your event everywhere you can. This is rarely true. Being all over the place might result in not covering any specific audience in-depth and not converting them to customers or event attendees in this case. Remember the Rule of Seven: a person should see or hear something seven times before they purchase and your followers on Instagram might be completely different from your LinkedIn crew, and your mailing list might have a different audience again. This doesn't mean that one of them is relevant and another one is not; it's up to you to decide. But we strongly advise you to focus most of your resources—money, time and others—on fewer channels. Run your targeted promotions well and reap the results on the event day.

Email marketing is a forever young marketing tool. According to Eventbrite data, delivery rates of mass emails are 98–99%, open rates are 25–40% and click-through rates are also 25–40%.

In our mobile world, you have to make sure it looks great on any smartphone or tablet, since over 50% will read your email from a mobile phone. You should also include visuals to make the message attractive and insert up to 5 links. Just don't get distracted from your core message.

Facebook is great for marketing B2C events, since you can target your audience very precisely. As it is a well-known demographics filter, you should definitely work with Facebook pixel, which is technically a code that's inserted to your website pages to track who your visitors were over a period of time. With this data you can create lookalike audiences and target them too!

Although LinkedIn ads might seem much more expensive than Facebook, this shouldn't scare you away from using it. Professional networks that you can reach out to via LinkedIn are of a different type and quality than those on any other social media. There are many ways you can tap into your audience via LinkedIn, so if your event has professional focus this is a tool to look at.

All of the above channels (and more!) can be used in a combination or separately. Don't feel too overwhelmed, you don't have to master all of them. Set your priorities and start working it!

EVENT WEBSITE AND SEO

Let's start with a question: do I need an event website?
Yes. Do you need a more detailed answer? Yes, of course you do.

In an industry survey of over 100,000 event attendees conducted by TicketBooth in 2017, 51% of people said they preferred buying tickets from an event website. There's so much more you can do with an event website than with a ticketing platform, and you'd better take advantage of this opportunity.

First and foremost, your own event website allows you to showcase your brand. Dynamic design, branded color schemes and visual effects are easily implemented via existing platforms and other online solutions can create an unforgettable experience for your potential attendees.

You can definitely answer more questions in a better manner if you're doing it on a personal website. The FAQ section is a basic part of your site that, again, can be implemented within a few hours of work, and it will help your guests prepare better too.

Besides, on your own website you can guide your customer through the experience of your future event and, eventually, win them over. Instead of kicking them out directly to the ticketing platform, you can show them more details, if you choose to do so, and showcase the bits and pieces that make your event stand out. The more excited your first customers are the quicker word of mouth spreads around and the better attendance you should expect.

Last but not least, your site can be integrated with Google analytics and Facebook via Facebook pixel. The latter gets you amazing insight into your customers' profiles even before you kick off the event. And the more time you dedicate to collecting this data the more accurate and detailed it is.

If you don't have a tech team in place, you don't need to dedicate enormous budgets to website making. Tools like Wix, Bizzabo and eTouches will help you create a beautifully designed event webpage in a day or less.

So now that you have taken the decision to go ahead with your event website, let's take a look at the three basic content principles of the website:
1 - simple
2 - dynamic
3 - optimized

Simplicity will help you showcase the most important details. Your visitors are much more likely to find what they are looking for if you arrange your site in a clear manner with less text at the very beginning of the page. Simplicity applies to both content and design. Try to keep it all clean and concise!

Dynamism will add some life to your page. Consider adding a countdown timer to the day of the event or to the last day of ticket sales to the main page. You can also show how many spots are still available if you have the technical capacity to do so.

Each piece of content of your website should make sense as a stand-alone piece and provide good value to readers. At the same time, it should all fall into the event canvas. If you meet these two criteria, search engines will give you a few extra points and you'll show higher. Better SEO means more visitors to the website, which means more visitors to your event!

Blogging is one of the recent favorite tools for content marketing. It's a great way to educate your audience on a topic of expertise, inform them about your event and get a chance to convert them. A popular format is lists: "10 ways to attract customers without cold-calling," "20 new business ideas in 2018,"and the like. Think of something that aligns well with your audience and your event topic and draft a few!

The other tool is video. You can introduce your speakers and showcase last year's speakers and attendees to create even more in-depth understanding of what's your event is about. If you already have some video content, there's no reason for you not to use it on your website. The truth is that people consume information in different ways, but currently the proportion who prefer audiovisuals to text is increasing. Cater for them and they'll come to you.

Organic search accounts for about 25% of visits to sites on the internet in general. So make sure that all this effort to create an amazing website doesn't end up going nowhere. You've got to make sure you're easy to discover. And now you've got a couple of tools for that already: your main page with all the information and your blog with several detailed and related pieces that are working towards your content marketing strategy and silently attracting visitors that are searching for the content on your topic.

On-page ranking factors are about your strategic choice of keywords. If your event is about real estate investment, make sure you place this phrase in your header, meta description and in general throughout the website. Don't exaggerate by using it in every single paragraph, but make sure it's well mentioned.

On-page links can also be helpful. For instance, if you need to give more information in another section of your site, inserting a link with a "Click here" description is not as useful as a link to "More on real estate investment."

Off-page ranking strategy consists of building a set of links on external websites that direct to your event website. It's a much tougher practice, it takes longer and is in general a bigger investment, but it's totally worth it if you've got a long-term strategy with your event. Here's how to do that. First and foremost, try to secure a few guest blog posts. As an expert in your industry, you can write about a topic related to your event and mention it in the piece. You've got to have an agreement in place in advance that active links are okay. A caveat: buying links used to be a well-used practice, but it's not what you should invest in now, not only because it's somewhat dodgy practice but merely because it's not bringing desired outcomes anymore. Websites linking to yours need to have similar topics but, most importantly, have a strong reputation. How can you check that? Look up their DA (domain authority) and other rankings on moz.com.

PROMOTING ON SOCIAL MEDIA

Paid advertising is great, but the initial organic boost you can get on social media is truly helpful. Your advertising can be much more successful if you "test the waters" first with organic reach and see which posts get more response with your audience. Besides, there are several other tools that you can try. Let's see what you can do to leverage social media and max out its potential.

- Turn your speakers into your promoters

They all have their followers, some more and others less. Creating visuals with their photo showcasing their expertise (branded, of course!) will transform a simple announcement of a speaker line-up into shareable material that can hit the news feed of your speaker's following.

- Go live

Social media is all about the "present moment", and no matter which tool you decide to concentrate on, it will have the option of "live video", so use it for quick updates, live interviews with your speakers, organizers—you name it. Live videos require minimal preparation, can be done in the interview format (you can stream your guest in) and will be saved for the future. You can download, edit and reuse them later on or just keep as basic live recordings on your feed. Your audience will appreciate extra content and information, so don't worry about imperfections, the notion of it being recorded live gives you many discounts.

- Use hashtags

In fact, "book" one hashtag for yourself! Check if it has been used before (ideally not), and promote the hashtag at your event and prior to it. Most event-related hashtags "explode" on the day of the event, so no worries if you've been pushing for everyone to hashtag your event while doing promotions and it's only the organizing team using it. Expect more mentions during your event. Also, check for an analytics platform to count the mentions for you. You can get some really interesting and helpful insights with this data.

- Create online communities

There are many tools, again, that you can use for community creation. Even months before the event day, you can create a Facebook, LinkedIn or Slack community to bring together your attendees and speakers (altogether or separately) and make them meet each other. Work on "tribe building" and it will pay back. In fact, making your people meet each other can take some workload off your shoulders: they can post questions to the community instead of your customer care, make travel arrangements between themselves and meet each other. In fact, ¾ of event attendees go to network, so your online community can be a highly demanded tool.

LANDING EVENT SPONSORS

Sponsorship strategy is a very important part of your event preparation, especially if you're dependent on sponsorship support to make your event happen. When I was organizing a sport event, our curators from the City Hall told me straight, "Land a big sponsorship partnership and only then continue planning the event." And they were right: if we hadn't had a big brand supporting our initiative, the event would have been impossible to organize. It wouldn't even have broken even without financial support from the big private company.

So, sometimes attracting the right sponsor is not only important, it's vital.

Let's break up your sponsor acquisition process into 4 parts:

A. Research your market players
B. Map their business objectives
C. Establish connections
D. Meet their goals

First of all, brainstorm who could be your potential sponsors. If you are organizing a history conference, maybe it's a niche publisher for textbooks, a company organizing archaeological tours, a producer of historical outfits or maybe an online portal that the audience of your future event uses on a daily basis? The ideas are endless. Try to put as many names down as you can.

As soon as your extensive list is ready, map your stakeholders with their business objectives. Not all sponsors are equal; in fact, they are all different. Big brands like Coca Cola or Vodafone might want to get a high level of exposure, whereas smaller local companies can be satisfied with a booth at your event or a commercial at the event opening. B2B companies might ask for business leads, B2C for promotion of their products or services.

Don't try to play a numbers game when reaching out to sponsors. Only talk to those you think you might help with your event. In fact, great collaborations are more sustainable and they work for longer than the one day of the event.

Once you know who's a good fit, it's time to research their contacts and reach out. Large companies can be reached through their press office or HR and smaller ones via a simple phone call to a founder or a managing director. Prepare your deck of slides about the event, personalize it and showcase the exact opportunities for them.

Meet their goals by proposing the type of activities they will like. Again, the outcome of the activities should bring the company to meet their business goals that you researched earlier when making your list. If it doesn't, then change the activity. If you can't, change the sponsor.

RESOURCES AND TOOLS

Great job finishing this book! Hopefully, you're now feeling a lot more confident about your upcoming event.

Here's a special thank you present.

As I mentioned in the very beginning, I'm making available my event checklist and event budgeting spreadsheet that you can download and customize.

Type this link in your browser and it will take you to the page where you can find both templates:
https://tinyurl.com/EventPlanningNinja

Have an amazing event and rock your business as a true Event Planning Ninja!